donnie darko

a collection of poems

by rebecca routh-sample

Other books by Rebecca Routh-Sample

*Fiction*

Diary Of A Teenage Fangirl

Diary Of A Teenage Rebel Girl

*Poetry*

ghost world

donnie darko

paramour

Spinner's End

All available to purchase on www.lulu.com

Connect with me on social media if you want! I'd love to hear your feedback:

Twitter: @itsbeccafy

Instagram: @beccafyofficial

TikTok: @itsbeccafy

Check out Amy's artwork:

Instagram: @amyleylaart

And buy her prints on Etsy:

www.etsy.com/uk/shop/PetrichorCorner

## contents

1. in the beginning
2. is it enough?
3. lemon and lime
4. best believe me
5. it's all part of the story.
6. i'm not leaving.
7. my only friend
8. rookie blue
9. marigolds
10. there's a letter that i never sent
11. indigo
12. time (non-linear)
13. justice league
14. my dying day
15. when I opened my eyes in a darkened room
16. chokehold

17. cage

18. come clean

19. zombie

20. lunada bay

21. move me

22. drag you down

23. babylon candle

24. altar

25. responsibility

26. end

**in the beginning**

in the beginning,

there was a girl

who wanted more than anything in the world to be loved

but she kept a secret

so big it consumed her

as hard as she tried, nobody really knew her.

in the beginning,

there was a girl

thrust into the big wide world

with wide eyes and white lies

and a love that turned you into gold,

if you were with her spirit you'd never grow old.

in the beginning,

there was love

two lovers that could change the world

bright lights, long nights

all they wanted was to be together.


in the beginning of it all,

two people met in secret

they did anything to keep it

and they didn't care if people understood.


cut your hair, change your mind

people do this all the time

tides change, waves break

minds change, hearts break

but no matter what


in the beginning there was love

and the world is always what it was

contrary as the tides that follow the moon.

i hope you'll get here soon,

because i want to be next to you.

**is it enough?**

all that i know

is you need me

beautiful damage

high waisted jeans

i love you

but i roll down my sleeves

because i don't

them to see the damage

of a love that was so, so wrong

but that's so so long

ago

what's in it gonna take?

my english rose

her nom de plume

and an empty home

devoid of furniture

but filled with love

we both have guardian

angels up above

you can see me

cause you've seen death

and bared

the brunt of the wilderness

and we've both almost

died

several times

there's a double meaning

on those little white lines

and i love you

is that enough?

my blonde baby

with that invisible touch

don't let the white noise drown

out

us

because nobody is taking

me away from you this

time

but is my love enough

is my love enough?

is my love enough?


what's it gonna take?

my brooklyn boy

lost in the island

of misfit toys

i can see you

cause i've seen death

so many times

it's starting to make sense

i wanna leave

but i won't go

because you

always bring me home

i know it's real this time

'cause we're grounded

with no yes men

and no 50 cents

we don't need your validation

don't know what's playing

on your radio station

we're on vacation

on a desert island

or in a blacked out

apartment

home is where the heart is

i love you

is my love enough?

when times get rough

times get hard

don't shut your eyes

just drive your car


is it enough?




**lemon and lime**


i like girls

i just think they're neat

just like marge simpson

with two left feet

girls

just breaking hearts

in paris

with left handed guitars

most of em

have such beautiful hearts

wear raspberry berets and

cry alone in their cars

listening to shakespeare's sister

on a lazy sunday

reading virgina woolfe

and drinking tea with honey

and i can call her

flower sugarplum or honey

and she always makes me laugh

'cause she's so damn funny

i can tell her all my secrets

she says its hunky

dory

like the david bowie album

handful of peach pits, cherries

some clementine

we listen to halsey

and drink some lemon and lime


i'm having such a great time

bathing in her light

i'm barefoot in the garden

drinking lemon and lime

i spin around

and kiss her time to time

and the world keeps spinning

and i'm absolutely fine

we're having such a great time

bathing in our light

we're barefoot in the garden

drinking lemon and lime

we spin around

and kiss each other

time after time

the world stops spinning

she's absolutely fine


never known a girl

that actually has

bette davis eyes

audrey hepburn in the morning

marilyn every night

amy winehouse in a jazz bar

annie when we fight

janelle when she makes me feel

lisa simpson

'cause she's always right


if you don't love women

more fool you

because there's nothing like

earning the respect of

a woman

and she's cool with you


act your age, not your shoe size

that's how you get the girl


**best believe me**

hurt me

you know you treat me badly

slap me

metaphorically

and happily

now it's proof

of the hatred

the bated breath

the fake shit

the misogyny

the damnation

bearing the brunt

of a broken up nation

and i don't give a flying

fuck

if England fucking wins

because i'm getting out of

here

and taking my damn kids

i carried them in my womb

so yes, they're fucking mine

and i'm leaving you

with old paperbacks and wine

beside your beer cans and lies

and best believe me

they'll be just fine


i held them in my arms

after a drawn out delivery

and i felt the tiny hands

and fingers

of my new born baby

the best thing that ever happened

to me

**it's all part of the story.**

take all of me

share your energy generously

i admire your generosity

you're my man

in this odyssey

and we'll meet endlessly and endlessly

and i'll always be everything

and you'll always be everything

blonde baby and my devilman

with the hands of a gentleman

bring it down

bring it down

i'm the sculptor and i'll sculpt it

it's all part of the story

we'll make our own odyssey

don't need anyone else to believe in me

don't need anyone else on earth to believe me


**i'm not leaving.**


i can't believe i ever let you in

just because you wanted to hit it

i can't believe

you have 2,000 soul ties

and you say it's none of my business

i can't believe you

have a broken heart but don't want to fix it

i can't believe

we had we had

and you don't even

miss it

listen

i'm not perfect

i know i'm a lot of work

listen

i'm not too naive to understand

you're sitting in a sitting in a lot of hurt

listen please

i'm not trying to

run in so hastily

i trip and fall

and trip some more

to the point my bags are

at your front door

boy, i'm sick of running

so i'm gonna sit down

gonna take off my slippers

and make myself a cup of tea

because you can't get rid of me that easily

so throw your worst at me

even if you want me to

i'm not leaving


so you can try all you want

boy

i'm not leaving

it's cold outside

and i'm not leaving.

**my only friend**

if i told you

life is fragile

would you believe me?

how could you

love a girl

who thinks this life is easy

i'm fine to die alone

i've made peace with

my broken bones

i'm fine in an empty home

well, i have to be

but i just think

if you ever did blink

and see the light

that reflects in the glass

in my kitchen sink

and knock on the door

while i'm on the brink

of a breakdown

and you come

round with your guard down

and your arms out

and you wrap me

up

inside your arms

and kiss me

we could start again

my only friend

my only friend

**rookie blue**

you make me see

life differently

it's like i had an epiphany

moved to york

at the age of 24

which heart full of gold

and a mouth that can talk

so much shit

it's my gift

Sagittarius, with a Taurus

rising for bliss

and an Aquarius moon

in a swimming pool

the mountain dew

the cobblestone streets

of magic

that blue sky is fantastic

i'm fed up of smog

filling my lungs

i wanna dress outrageous

and have some fun

i want to love each other

like were the only ones

in the universe

it's almost if i imagined her

rookie blue


you studied film

and i studied pain

i made you dance

all in the rain

we lived together

only just

paying the rent

collecting dust

sharing trust

moved in our stuff

unpacked the baggage

had a look

we moved on

and the moonlight struck

us

while we're dancing

outside the everyman

waiting for the bus

like we owned the universe

it was as if i imagined her

rookie blue


**marigolds**

if you ever want to call, though

standing at the crossroads

i've been up all

night

taking me a long time

you can have my phone

and you can have my passcode

you can have my paypal

you can have my soul

you can have this ring

and my hand to have and hold

side by side

in a shallow grave

covered in marigolds



**there's a letter i never sent**

there's a letter i never sent

in the photo frame on the eft

there's a letter in never sent

backstage on a saturday night

alive with the regret

there's money i never spent

on a flat i'd never rent

and in the door is a dent

from a fight we never had

where you never left

there's so many missed bullets

i'll never have the time to repent

giving my bad attitude up for lent

been saying that for about a decade

and it's exactly what i meant

i keep you in a locket

my true love, my only friend

all the time we didn't spend

in a letter i never sent

**indigo**

trying not to feel the pain

dragging me down into the earth

painful, painful, painful

all it does is hurt

what's the point of being

star-crossed?

if you're that hungry for fame

a Gryffindor embracing

a Slytherin

while a Hufflepuff sadly waits

take a shard of glass

hold it firmly to my face

curse myself for loving you

hate having to wait

jealous, deep like indigo

lips covered in plum

waiting in my car

ace of spades joking around

on the queen of hearts

all of this is becoming dreadfully

redundant

like what's the fucking point

wildflowers on my phone case

an ache in all my joints

you're a fucking lunatic

and so am i at this point

**time (non-linear)**

blue was the colour of

the love you put me through

time is non-linear but

it's jagged with you

tried to use occam's razor

but nothing's simple with you

it just let me with my skin

all cut into

'i love yous' turn into 'fuck yous'

and sweet nothings to revenge

diamond rings to daggers

lovers into friends

i thought looking at a photograph

would take me back to that place

but i don't look the same anymore

time passes like an opera with

three different interludes

beginning, middle, end

it's boring

and if you think i'm going to sit through it

you're delusional

girls only have so much time

before they have to choose

in a race with biology

over the first couple hurdles

before it occurs to you

by the time you've decided to make the decision to choose

we're over the finish line

and walking away with

a trophy and someone new

you watch me as i walk away

into that tangerine sunset

you whisper 'i'm fine'

but you're lying

and there's nobody there to hear you

**justice league**

if a picture paints a thousand words

a mugshot paints a dozen

a son from an illustrious father

i thought i might be your cousin


your eyes are black, there's nothing there

can't remember a time where i used to care

you walk on the stage in underwear

you talk in riddles and lies

you think you're profound and prophetic

but you're the exact thing you claim to despise

on your hands, blood and far too much time

you've been given so many chances

from the age of seventeen

you're a late-twenties nightmare

you used to be my teenage dream

i really, really thought

there was something we didn't see

something that expressed the madness that flowed into your poetry

i thought there was magic and lightning

now you're just frightening

and you're proving them all right

you know you're proving them right, right?

your music is shit but your eyeliner's worse

wish you had a reality check in your second-hand purse

i hate you for what you did to me

and what you did to her

and her

and her

a privileged white man with little to lose and everything to gain

over-zealous, self-indulgent and quite frankly insane


i miss the days where i'd defend you

like a superhero

but there's simply no justice

and i'm out of your league

baby, just go

just go



**my dying day**


my daddy left on a monday

he said 'see you on tuesday'

and i didn't see him for a decade

and by the time he came back

i'd already given myself away

to a man who said he'd never

do the same


and my daughter said

my daddy left on a monday

he said 'see you on tuesday'

and i didn't see him for a decade


and then her therapist

said 'that's quite a story'

and put her pen away

and she said

my daddy left on a monday

he said 'see you on tuesday'

and i didn't see him for a decade

and by the time he came back

it was already too late

i didn't need anyone

my pathology had pathologised

my self-sufficient state


and her grave said

my daddy left on a monday

he said 'see you on tuesday'

i didn't need him

i didn't need anyone

'til my dying day



**when i opened my eyes in a darkened room**


when i opened my eyes in a darkened room

artefacts of adolescence

judy bloom

where you're no longer 15

but not quite 25

where do you exactly fit in life?

desolate longing

drowning in regret

wounds that you caught

in the wilderness

that willow lead me to straight to you

i ate the forbidden fruit

apples, cherries, peach pits

face wipes, brushes and lip kits

overdue homework and

stolen kisses

you blink just enough to miss it

i hope that you would visit

because i see you in my dreams

all the time

a different timeline

i just say i'm fine

they ask why

and

i just say i'm fine



**chokehold**


you wake up with a bad throat

caught in a chokehold

from a man sitting on a throne

of brittle bones

and illusions


i thought i could change

myself to be the one

be better in everything i've done

twisted myself to a pretzel

trying to earn your love

chasing you, but i found myself

and if you weren't a criminal

i'd wish you well


can't let myself get down with this


paint your face

and masquerade

but you're as subtle

as your imaginary barricade


you were once my dream

now i can't breathe


cupid, let me go

let me out of this chokehold

**cage**

cage

held hostage by their rage

locked in by the game

disheartened by the rules they make

victim of circumstance

taking the fall for others' mistakes

emancipated because you can't be tamed

so you take the stage

and work your way to glory

whilst you're locked in their cage

and the worst part is the players think they're free

but they are victims of their forefathers tyranny

they think they think outside of the box

but there is no greater knowledge than love

and the demons of their grandfather's fathers

keep them eternally stuck


turns out we're all held in a greater cage

we're all players in a game that plays itself

there is no winning or losing

only hell


throw away the rules

leave the game

fold up the board, put it away

name it by its' true name

and don't hide the box away

leave it all to see

remind ourselves of how foolish we have been

think its been a long time, and playing games has grown quite weary

let's decide to love ourselves

accept the truth that we are fearing

the only true love is agape

if that makes you a-gape

you've gone astray

let's leave this lesson for today

why would anyone want to be captive in their own cage?

**come clean**

you won't answer my calls

i'm talking to the wall

everyone can hear me screaming

but i'm far too easy to ignore

been gaslighted so many times i call you a fire starter

been hurt so much i can't feel it anymore, please just hit me harder


living in a bell jar

screaming into the abyss

living in an eco chamber

of the taste of our last kiss

i don't want to pressure you

but i wouldn't mind some haste

if you don't respond by twilight

the truth I'll have to face


you're a lying cheating heathen with a penchant for pain

you're a selfish greedy hedonist who makes their prey insane

you're a hunter in the wilderness with a taste for other's blood

you're a conscious addict who pretends they're misunderstood

come clean? get clean?

I wish you would

the years pass like the November wind

and i heal from the comatose state you put me in

it's exhausting chasing dragons when you're not in a fairytale

grounded in reality, a monotone betrayal

i cracked open the bell jar

escaped into the light

i live in a rainbow prism

a true heart's only right

to live in a world of people

who give more than they take

with hindsight I stay strong

look back on my mistakes

i didn't think it would end this badly

but I did it to myself

i need to come clean

i should've made you get some help

the burden of another's strife

is too heavy to ignore

but too much to tackle alone

when they're one foot out the door

moral of the story: you don't need to be in love

better to be alone, than love the cage that traps the dove


come clean, admit you did all you can

and once you've learned that lesson you don't need to look back



**zombie**


i'm a zombie

i'm the walking dead

pilled up to the eyeballs

life hanging by a thread

and it wouldn't be a lie to say you're my only friend

and it wouldn't be a lie to say the feelings I feel for you are the only feelings I have left

and every night I lie in the dark with a weight in my heart

and a sharp shooting pain in my chest because I know I ruined everything, because that's all I do

and I run away because I'm scared of what's left.

we can't be friends

but we can't be lovers

and the sight of you drives me mad.


not because I hate you,

not because you did anything bad...

because it's my fault you'll never love me back.

**lunada bay**

she smelled of lunada bay

i asked her if she'd take me there some day

she said 'on this side of paradise there is no doubt

but on the other it's only paranoia

when there's someone you can't live without'


lakeside blue azure sparkle like your eyes

hot on my ski

sweat on your sweatshirt

you listen to earl put your feet up like they hurt

i like that one song that makes it all makes sense

but then it all goes wrong after you confess

and you try to figure out what it all meant

when you still smell the mist of her body in your bed

**move me**

i would sit by my phone

hang on your every word

but every time you take a day to reply

is a lesson learned

i used to linger on your every move, because they were so beautiful

and so very you


i used to move you and you still move me

mostly to tears and you've forgotten me

i'll tell that to you next time we meet

but I'm certain it will only be in dreams


you don't move me anymore,

you just make me sick.

i used to think you were John the Baptist, now I realise you're full of shit.

you don't move me anymore quite frankly, i feel still.

if you're still trippin' over this, mate, you just need to chill.

**drag you down**

my waters are blue and dark

will you save me from drowning?

or were you just looking for a pond

pretty and easy to clean

well i'm sorry i'm so deep

find someone shallow next time

or just look were you're going or swim in someone else

because these eels are choking me and its hard to breathe

so keep my pearl precious and ask you to leave

sorry I dragged you down with me,

i'm not sorry actually i can't stop being me.

**babylon candle**

i'll take you home like a babylon

candle

i'll take you home

even if it's not with me

i'll take you home like a babylon

candle

even if it's not with me

even if it's to me

but they come after you

over the wall

where the mad shit happens

i feel the need to defend you

i'll do the right thing

loyal to the core

and i'll keep my candle burning

as long as your heart keeps

beating

i don't care who it's beating for

your life is the only thing i'd care to fight for


i'm not aggressive

i'm not abrasive

but if you come after

someone i love

you're dead

let's face it


take me home

like a babylon candle

even if you're home isn't with me

even if it's not with me


**altar**

i am an item, a service well bought

dressed up in silk

and so I am taught:

'anatomy is destiny',

the silkworms say

i don't know what I'd say if I had my way

and the silkworms they worm their way into my skin

turn me into something beautiful from the outside in

i've lived with no choices, i've lived insecure

only to be the sickly sweet peach, demure

of the martyrs i slated i don't know what i'd say

they jumped in front of charging stallions

my parents gave me away


picked out from a prison line-up

i'm saved by chastity

saved?

i'm a pig to the slaughter

blood drips slowly from the altar

velvet stream


i don't know my partner

but I'll know them well enough

and by the time i do

i will not be able to leave and pack up

cover your eyes, modesty modesty

sometimes i feel this silk is a curtain of animosity

i ask: 'why do you hate me?'

but they all scream: 'we love you!'

today I'm sacrificed at the altar

for the sake of honor and virtue

**responsibility**

stop it

i don't wanna stop it

i don't wanna be here

i don't wanna drop it

i'm not gonna do it just cause you tell me to

i'm not gonna break

just cause you bend me to

stop telling women

what to fucking do

i'm over it right now

i'm not letting go of my pain

i'm not by definition malleable

and i'm not wallpapering over

paint

just so you don't have to feel my pain

why is it always my

fucking responsibility

why are children

my responsibility

why is emotional labour

my responsibility

why is beauty

my

responsibility

why are your

shortcomings

my responsibility

why do you want me

to lie

and tell you i love you

when you i can't even stand

to look at you


no, no, no.


**end**


i don't want this to end

i want us to sincerely always be friends

the balls in your court it all depends

if you let it fade away,

or it if you won't let it end.

we were babes in the wood, too young to make sense

we'd crumble under pressure

burnt under the lense.

you were friends with the bad kids,

but I held your heart,

and it wouldn't have mattered until they tore you apart

but i kissed your wounds and tied your arm with a scarf

and i let you kept your heart heavy

but i let you feel sparks,

and you shone like the stars.


twice we broke up, twice we regret

so in the library that's were we met

we sent notes in classrooms and I won't forget

the stories we made and the lies that we met

i'd worry about everything,

i'd always fret

you couldn't stand it but that's what you get

and if you weren't on my team

i wouldn't know who I was playing for

i wouldn't have a key if you hadn't opened the door

because i'd never been there before.


why can't you hold me like you used to?

why can't you smell me on your used suit?

why wasn't I there for you?

why are we risking it all falling through?

why can't you remember the things I tell you?

why are you soaring free like a bird?

there's no point in one of flying if one of us is hurt,

and i'm hurt.


meet me with your top hat,

and let's play pretend

teach me that true love never ends

i'll wear a nice dress

tell all your friends

your heart is a wonderland where love never ends.